A WESLEY BIBLE STUDY

GUIDE
by
M. Kathryn
Armistead

JAMES W. MOORE

How God Takes Our Little & Makes It Much

IDEAL FOR USE WITH
The WESLEY STUDY BIBLE

Abingdon Press
NASHVILLE

HOW GOD TAKES OUR LITTLE AND MAKES IT MUCH
LEADER'S GUIDE

Copyright © 2010 by Abingdon Press

This book is printed on acid-free paper.

Library of Congress Cataloging-in-Publication Data

ISBN 978-1-4267-0879-4

Scripture quotations are from the New Revised Standard Version of the Bible, copyright 1989, Division of Christian Education of the National Council of the
Churches of Christ in the United States of America. Used by permission. All rights
reserved.

10 11 12 13 14 15 16 17 18 19—10 9 8 7 6 5 4 3 2 1

MANUFACTURED IN THE UNITED STATES OF AMERICA

CONTENTS

A WORD TO LEADERS:
HOW TO USE THIS RESOURCE 5

Session 1: God Takes a Reluctant Shepherd
and Makes a Bold Leader:
The Story of Moses 13

Session 2: God Takes a Harem Girl and Makes a
Heroine: *The Story of Esther* 22

Session 3: God Finds the Lost and Celebrates
with Joy: *The Lost Sheep,
the Lost Coin, and the Lost Son* 29

Session 4: God Takes a Fisherman and Makes a
Disciple for All People:
The Story of Peter 40

Session 5: God Takes Our Little and
Makes It Much:
The Story of the Church 50

Session 6: God Takes Mere Sinners and
Makes Us *More* than Conquerors 61

A WORD TO LEADERS: HOW TO USE THIS RESOURCE

*H*ow God Takes Our Little and Makes It Much by James Moore is a six-week video-based study for adult groups. The goal of this study is to help participants engage significant biblical persons as presented in key Scripture passages. Then, after thoughtful self-examination, persons are invited to dialogue in a small-group setting, so that their lives will be enriched and they can be more fruitful followers of Jesus.

Dr. Moore invites you to help readers put their faith into daily practice, so that they will be inspired to share God's grace with others. As disciples practicing their faith, they will better understand and feel good about their distinctive Wesleyan identity. Many of these basic practices are spelled out in the *Life Applications Topics* and *Core Terms* found in the *Wesley Study Bible*.

As group leader, you are invited to facilitate each session using this leader's guide. You will need a copy of the book *How God Takes Our Little and Makes It Much* and, for best results, a *Wesley Study Bible* for each participant, and a chart or board with appropriate writing instruments for group activities.

Throughout the book, Dr. Moore refers to the *Life Application Topics* and *Core Terms* that appear as sidebars within the notes of the *Wesley Study Bible*. For your convenience, *Life Application Topics* and *Core Terms* are listed by biblical book and in alphabetical order in the back of the *Wesley Study Bible*. Just as John Wesley sought to speak as plainly as possible, these brief explanations will help people live with warmed hearts and active hands.

You, as leader, might want to make a list of the *Life Application Topics* and *Core Terms* referred to in each chapter and read them ahead of time. They will be a valued resource for you as you study, plan, and lead the sessions. They will also help you keep the discussion focused.

Each chapter has points designed to help people live out their faith in their daily lives. In addition, each chapter also has a "Biblical Perspective" to help persons go a step deeper. Here readers will find additional passages of Scripture with thoughtful commentary.

A Quick Overview

Because no two groups are alike, this guide has been designed to give you flexibility in tailoring the sessions to your needs. You may use the following suggested format, *or adapt it as you wish to meet the schedule and needs of your particular group.* (Note: The times indicated within parentheses are merely estimates. You may move at a faster or slower pace, making adjustments as necessary to fit your schedule.)

Suggested Format	**(45-65 minutes)**
Sharing Prayers and Concerns	(5-7 minutes)
Opening Prayer	(1-2 minutes)
Introduction of Study	(2-3 minutes)
Play DVD	(5-10 minutes)
Icebreaker	(10 minutes)
Scripture Reading	(3-5 minutes)
Group Discussion	(20-25 minutes)
Closing Prayer	(1-2 minutes)

Helpful Hints

Here are a few helpful hints for preparing and leading your group sessions: Read the corresponding chapter in *How God Takes Our Little and Makes It Much* before the group session. Make note of the Scripture references.

- Select the specific discussion questions you plan to cover. Highlight these or put a checkmark beside them. (For 20-25 minutes of discussion time, it is suggested that you select 5-7 questions.)

- Be the first person at the session. Arrive at least five minutes early so you can welcome persons as they come in. Practice gracious hospitality.
- Begin and end on time.
- Make sure to introduce guests and help them feel welcome.
- Keep the business of the group short.
- Be enthusiastic. Remember, you set the tone for the class.
- Create a climate of participation, encouraging individuals to participate in ways that are comfortable for them.
- Some people are uncomfortable talking, so occasionally let them write their responses. If no one answers at first, don't be afraid of a little silence. Count to seven silently; then say something such as, "Would anyone like to go first?" If no one responds, venture an answer yourself. Have your answer prepared ahead of time. Then ask for comments and other responses.
- Model openness as you share with the group. Group members will follow your example. If you only share at a surface level, everyone else will follow suit. If you want a richer discussion, you need to share at a deeper level yourself.

- Be aware, however, that it is natural for the conversation to begin at a surface level and then move more deeply as the session goes on.
- Draw out participants without asking them to share what they are unwilling to share. Make eye contact with someone and say something such as, "How about someone else?"
- Encourage multiple responses before moving on. If you want more conversation around a response, ask something like, "Has that ever happened to anyone else?"
- If you have trouble getting responses from the group, consider giving your answer first and then just going around the circle.
- Avoid asking "Why?" or "Why do you believe that?" Instead consider asking or giving an example to illustrate the point.
- Affirm others' responses with comments such as, "Great," or "Thanks," or "I like that"—especially if this is the first time someone has spoken during the group session.
- Steer the conversation away from argument. If you feel things heating up, say something like, "You seem to feel strongly about this."
- Give everyone a chance to talk but keep the conversation moving. Moderate the group to prevent

a few individuals from doing all of the talking. Please note that some people will not talk unless you call on them.

- Monitor your own contributions. If you are doing most of the talking, back off.

- Remember that you do not have to have all the answers. Your job is to keep the discussion going and encourage participation.

- Honor the time schedule. If a session is running longer than expected, get consensus from the group before continuing beyond the agreed-upon ending time.

- Consider involving group members in various aspects of the group session, such as asking for volunteers to read Scripture, the closing prayer, or to say their own prayer, and so forth. Prayers are included in this guide if you need to make copies ahead of time.

- Before each group session and throughout the study, pray for God's presence, guidance, and power. Pray for your group members by name and for what God may do in their lives. More than anything else, prayer will encourage and empower you as you lead the group.

It takes a dedicated leader to make any group go well.

Thank you for your commitment. Blessings on your ministry.

A Prayer for You, the Leader

Dear Holy God, thank you for the opportunity of leadership. It is an awesome task to help persons along their spiritual journey. Help this leader follow your Spirit in preparation for each session. Give this leader confidence and a humble spirit. Empower this leader to speak with your words, listen with your ears, and see with your eyes. Give this leader insight to inspire learning and more faithful living. Let this leader find the joy of your salvation. In Jesus' name, amen.

Before You Meet

Prior to your first group session, pray for the members of your group by name. Pray that the study will touch them in a significant way and that you will be a helpful conduit of God's grace. Pray that they will be eager to learn and grow into the image of Christ. Pray that they will be faithful in their own study and purposeful in their daily living.

Call members prior to your first meeting to personally remind them that the group is beginning this new study. Invite them to participate and, perhaps, bring a new person to the group. You might explain that is it always easier for new people to come if the group is beginning something new. You might also tell your group members that you've already read the entire book and how much you like it.

Consider having a special kick-off session with refreshments. Perhaps you'd like to meet in a special place or go somewhere afterwards as a group to celebrate beginning a new opportunity to grow in Christian discipleship. Or you might consider planning a special mission project that reflects how God can take our little and make it much.

Session 1

God Takes a Reluctant Shepherd and Makes a Bold Leader: The Story of Moses

Leader Preparation

Read chapter 1 in *How God Takes Our Little and Makes It Much*. Look through this session and decide which discussion questions will work best for your group. If the suggested questions need modification, please feel free to make the desired changes.

Leader Extra

Moses: According to *The New Interpreter's Dictionary of the Bible*, Moses is the first great leader of the people of Israel. In him, we see characteristics of a founding ruler, judge, law-giver, scribe, teacher, prophet, intercessor, healer, and savior. He led Israel out of slavery in Egypt in the exodus (Exodus 14–15), spoke "face to face" with God (Exodus 33:11; Numbers 12:8; Deuteronomy 34:10), and transmitted the Ten Commandments and other laws from God on Mount Sinai to the Israelites (Exodus 19–20). Even today, Moses retains his prominence and importance in both Jewish and Christian imaginations.

God called Moses to lead Israel out of slavery in Exod 3. Exodus 3 has similarities to other stories in the Bible in which a person is called to be a prophet or deliverer. When God commands Moses, Moses responds with five objections. First, Moses claims to lack adequate qualification, but God assures him that "I will be with you" (3:11-12). Second, the Israelites will ask Moses for God's name, so God gives a name that is both substantive but also elusive—"I AM WHO I AM" (3:13-14). Third, Moses worries that the Israelites will not believe that God has sent him. So God gives Moses two signs or wonders (4:1-9). Fourth, Moses objects that he is not eloquent, but God assures him that God will teach him what to say (4:10-12). And fifth, Moses simply begs God to send someone else. So God also sends Aaron. These five objections serve as a kind of theology of leadership. They underscore the frailty of leaders and their constant need for God.

In this session, consider your own strengths and weaknesses. Consider how you can help the participants become more willing to follow where God leads. Pray that God will guide and strengthen you as you lead this small group study.

Getting Started

Sharing Prayers and Concerns (5-7 minutes)

Opening Prayer (1-2 minutes)

Dear God, we long to meet you face to face, but sometimes we are afraid. Like Moses, we make excuses. While we pray to make a difference in this world, sometimes it just feels like the challenges are too threatening and intimidating. Help us realize that you know our name. You have a purpose for us. Help us lean on your faithful promise to always be with us. Thank you for your faithfulness to us even when we are not as faithful as we need to be. But even when we turn from you, you are there, pursuing us with your ever-seeking love. Be with those persons we've mentioned. Let them feel the presence of your Holy Spirit. But help us also do our part to assist and comfort them. Now we turn our hearts to you. Touch us, inspire us, lead us so that we might see just a glimpse of your glory. In Jesus' name, amen.

Introduction of Study (2-3 minutes)

To the leader: Take a few minutes to introduce this session.

In this chapter, God takes Moses, the shepherd and former runaway Egyptian prince, and makes him into a great leader. James Moore gives us three thoughts that emerge from the story of Moses in the book of Exodus. First, when we have to face the pharaohs of life, we can remember that the name of God is "I Shall Be There." Second, when we have to wander in the wilderness, we can remember that the name if God is "I Shall Be There." Third, when we have to face death, we can remember that the name of God is "I Shall Be There."

Play the DVD: Session 1 (5-10 minutes)

Icebreaker (10 minutes)

Moses noticed the burning bush and found God.

What do you notice first when you meet people? Their eyes, handshake, clothes, the shine on their shoes? What kind of first impression do you like to make?

Scripture Reading (3-5 minutes)

Exodus 3:1-20

Moses was keeping the flock of his father-in-law Jethro, the priest of Midian; he led his flock beyond the wilderness, and came to Horeb, the mountain of God. There the angel of the LORD appeared to him in a flame of fire out of a bush; he looked, and the bush was blazing, yet it was not consumed. Then Moses said, "I must turn aside and look at this great sight, and see why the bush is not burned up." When the LORD saw that he had turned aside to see, God called to him out of the bush, "Moses, Moses!" And he said, "Here I am." Then he said, "Come no closer! Remove the sandals from your feet, for the place on which you are standing is holy ground." He said further, "I am the God of your father, the God of Abraham, the God of Isaac, and the God of Jacob." And Moses hid his face, for he was afraid to look at God.

Then the LORD said, "I have observed the misery of my people who are in Egypt; I have heard their cry on account of their taskmasters. Indeed, I know their sufferings, and I have come down to deliver them from the Egyptians, and to bring them up out of that land to a good and broad land, a land flowing with milk and honey, to the country of the Canaanites, the Hittites, the Amorites, the Perizzites, the Hivites, and the Jebusites. The cry of the Israelites has now come to me; I have also seen how the Egyptians oppress them. So come, I will send you to Pharaoh to bring my people, the Israelites, out of Egypt." But Moses said to God, "Who am I that I should go to Pharaoh, and bring the Israelites out of Egypt?" He said, "I will be with you; and this shall be the sign for you that it is I who sent you: when you have brought the people out of Egypt, you shall worship God on this mountain."

But Moses said to God, "If I come to the Israelites and say to them, 'The God of your ancestors has sent me to you,' and they ask me, 'What is his name?' what shall I say to them?" God said to Moses, "I AM WHO I AM." He said further, "Thus you shall say to the Israelites, 'I AM has sent me to you.' " God also said to Moses, "Thus you shall say to the Israelites, 'The LORD, the God of your ancestors, the God of Abraham, the God of Isaac, and the God of Jacob, has sent me to you':

This is my name forever,

and this my title for all generations.

Go and assemble the elders of Israel, and say to them, 'The LORD, the God of your ancestors, the God of Abraham, of Isaac, and of Jacob, has appeared to me, saying: I have given heed to you and to what has been done to you in Egypt. I declare that I will bring you up out of the misery of Egypt, to the land of the Canaanites, the Hittites, the Amorites, the Perizzites, the Hivites, and the Jebusites, a land flowing with milk and honey.' They will listen to your voice; and you and the elders of Israel shall go to the king of Egypt and say to him, 'The LORD, the God of the Hebrews, has met with us; let us now go a three days' journey into the wilderness, so that we may sacrifice to the LORD our God.' I know, however, that the king of Egypt will not let you go unless compelled by a mighty hand. So I will stretch out my hand and strike Egypt with all my wonders that I will perform in it; after that he will let you go."

Exodus 33:19

And he said, "I will make all my goodness pass before you, and will proclaim before you the name, 'The LORD'; and I will be gracious to whom I will be gracious, and will show mercy on whom I will show mercy."

Joshua 1:5-9

"No one shall be able to stand against you all the days of your life. As I was with Moses, so I will be with you; I will not fail you or forsake you. Be strong and courageous; for you shall put this people in possession of the land that I swore to their ancestors to give them. Only be strong and very courageous, being careful to act in accordance with all the law that my servant Moses commanded you; do not turn from it to the right hand or to the left, so that you may be successful wherever you go. This book of the law shall not depart out of your mouth; you shall meditate on it day and night, so that you may be careful to act in accordance with all that is written in it. For then you shall make your way prosperous, and then you shall be successful. I hereby command you: Be strong and courageous; do not be frightened or dismayed, for the LORD your God is with you wherever you go."

Psalm 23

The LORD is my shepherd, I shall not want.

He makes me lie down in green pastures;
he leads me beside still waters;
he restores my soul.
He leads me in right paths
for his name's sake.
Even though I walk through the darkest valley,
I fear no evil;
for you are with me;
your rod and your staff—
they comfort me.
You prepare a table before me
in the presence of my enemies;
you anoint my head with oil;
my cup overflows.
Surely goodness and mercy shall follow me

all the days of my life,
and I shall dwell in the house of the LORD
my whole life long.

Group Discussion (20-25 minutes)

1. People put their faith in all kinds of ordinary things, for example: car brakes, the availability of candy bars, and gravity. Share a time when you put your faith in someone or a time when someone put their faith in you. How easy is it for you to put faith in God's extraordinary love for you?

2. Who have been some of your faithful guides—a spouse, teacher, coworker, pastor, friend, child? How did they show you what it means to love God and neighbor? What did they do and what did you learn from them?

3. What are the Pharaohs that you are facing in your life now? A relationship, a situation at work, a boss, an illness, a family problem, a financial concern? Take a few minutes and write down the obstacles Moses faced and what Moses feared.

4. For most people it is hard to talk about things that frighten or intimidate them. In your experience, what is it like to be intimidated by a bully? How should we deal with bullies? When do you just walk away?

5. Where do you especially need God present with you today?

6. It is said that when God closes a door, God opens a window. Share a time when God came through for you.

7. God's name can be translated and understood in many ways. "I Shall Be There for You" and "I AM WHO I AM" are two. What difference does it make how we understand God's name? If Jesus is a name for God, what does that name say about who God is for us?

8. Where do you need God's grace to be bold? With whom do you need to share God's love today? Think of a relationship in your life that needs some work. What can you do to let the love of God show through you to that person?

Closing Prayer (1-2 minutes)

Dear God, out of the burning bush you proclaimed your name to Moses. Your name describes your promise to always be with us. Lord, we need you to help us face our fears, challenges, and obstacles. Sometimes you are the only one who is urging us to go forward. Yours is the only positive voice we hear. We need your steadfast, loving kindness. Help us see the burning bushes you have for us. Help us take time to turn aside and see your glory. Help us not give up but strive toward your purpose. Thank you for loving us—now empower us to follow you more faithfully. In Jesus' name, amen.

Session 2

God Takes a Harem Girl and Makes a Heroine: The Story of Esther

Leader Preparation

Read chapter 2 in *How God Takes Our Little and Makes It Much.* Look through this session and decide which discussion questions will work best for your group. If the suggested questions need modification, please feel free to make the desired changes.

Leader Extra

Esther: In the book of Esther, we are told that Esther was an orphan adopted by her cousin Mordecai. According to *The New Interpreter's Dictionary of the Bible*, Esther appears as one of the many virgin girls rounded up as a potential replacement for the exiled Queen Vashti. Esther is singled out by the eunuch Hegia (2:9, 15). But Esther's emergence as a person in her own right occurs as she moves toward the strategic revelation of her Jewishness to King Ahasuerus and to Mordecai's mortal enemy, Haman. In the end Esther finds a way to shift her situation to her advantage and to the advantage of all her people, thereby becoming their deliverer.

The book of Esther is set in the Persian Empire. It describes the Jews' endangerment and subsequent deliverance from the genocide plotted against them. This happy ending is brought about through Esther's initiative and ingenuity. Despite the intriguing story, however, readers throughout history have wondered about the book's theological importance. God is not active in the events nor is God mentioned. In addition, other elements typical of biblical literature that might suggest religious interest are also not present, for example, prayer, temple worship, covenant language. Yet many persons find that God acts in a similar way in their own lives—through circumstance—and where we can see only in retrospect how God was at work.

As you prepare this session, think about the times you have been in the minority. Perhaps you held a minority opinion or were an outsider in a group. Reflect how there are sometimes advantages of being in the minority or an outsider. Also consider your small group, who are the insiders and outsiders? How might this affect how you lead the group?

Getting Started

Sharing Prayers and Concerns (5-7 minutes)

Opening Prayer (1-2 minutes)

Dear God, we know you stand for what is true, merciful, and righteous. You showed us through the life of your Son, Jesus Christ. And you also showed us through the lives of people like Esther, Jacob, and Daniel. While we did not choose to be born at this time or in this place, help us make the most of what we've been given, so that we can truly make a difference in this world.

Today, we celebrate your love, power, and justice; and we especially thank you for your active, initiating, and ever-seeking love. We know that in the tough times, we can count on your promises to heal, guide, reconcile, and sustain us. Bless those whom we have mentioned, and let us now lift our hearts and turn our eyes upon you. In Jesus' name, amen.

Introduction of Study (2-3 minutes)

To the leader: Take a few minutes to introduce this session.

In this chapter, Dr. Moore shows how God took Esther, a harem girl with a cloudy future, and made a heroine. Esther was heroic because she seized the moment, expressed sacrificial love, and stood tall for her faith and helped others.

Play the DVD: Session 2 (5-10 minutes)

Icebreaker (10 minutes)

Share a time when you or someone you know was at the right place at the right time—perhaps to meet a special person, secure that hard-to-get job, or meet that impossible goal. Was it luck, God, or something else? What do you think? Do you believe in luck?

Scripture Reading (3-5 minutes)

Esther 4:1-7

When Mordecai learned all that had been done, Mordecai tore his clothes and put on sackcloth and ashes, and went through the city, wailing with a loud and bitter cry; he went up to the entrance of the king's gate, for no one might enter the king's gate clothed with sackcloth. In every province, wherever the king's command and his decree came, there was great mourning among the Jews, with fasting and weeping and lamenting, and most of them lay in sackcloth and ashes.

When Esther's maids and her eunuchs came and told her, the queen was deeply distressed; she sent garments to clothe Mordecai, so that he might take off his sackcloth; but he would not accept them. Then Esther called for Hathach, one of the king's eunuchs, who had been appointed to attend her, and ordered him to go to Mordecai to learn what was happening and why. Hathach went out to Mordecai in the open square of the city in front of the king's gate, and Mordecai told him all that had happened to him, and the exact sum of money that Haman had promised to pay into the king's treasuries for the destruction of the Jews.

Daniel 6:22

"My God sent his angel and shut the lions' mouths so that they would not hurt me, because I was found blameless before him; and also before you, O king, I have done no wrong."

Group Discussion (20-25 minutes)

1. Esther became queen because she replaced Vashti, the former queen. Share a time when you had to follow someone at a job or when you replaced someone, for example, on a project. How does the person you follow affect the expectations that are placed on you?

2. Esther was heroic because she seized the moment. Share a time when you or someone you know seized the moment. What does it take to seize the moment?

3. Teens often tell their parents that, "It is a new day. Things aren't the way they used to be," or words to that effect. How has the world changed in the last ten years, the last twenty years, the last fifty years? In what ways is the world the same?

4. Do you believe that you are living the life that God intends for you? Are there things in your life that you believe God is calling you to do today? If a person's relationships are shaped by love, what are the characteristics of that loving relationship? For example, how do you listen, how do you show you care, how do you set aside time for another person?

5. John Wesley had a life-changing experience at Aldersgate, in London, England. There, according to his own words, his heart was "strangely warmed." Share a time when you had a heartwarming experience. Share what happened to you or someone you know when

you or that person had a life-changing experience. How old were you? Where were you? What were the long-term consequences?

6. Esther was heroic because she expressed sacrificial love. How have you sacrificed for your loved ones? What is the difference between giving sacrificial love and being a doormat? When you make sacrifices, what do you expect in return? Nothing, gratitude, sacrifices in return, love?

7. Some people are simply hard to love; for example, someone who has hurt you or someone you love. Jesus says that we are to love our enemies. What does that really mean?

8. Joseph says that what you meant for evil, God meant for good. What happened to Joseph and when did he say this? Are there times in your life when God turned a tragedy into a triumph?

9. Daniel ended up in the lion's den. Are you facing any lions in your life right now? How can God help you? What do you need to ask for from yourself, others, God?

10. Esther was a hero; she was a success. Who are your heroes and what do they say about who you are? Where do you need success right now in your life, in the life of your family, in the life of your church?

Closing Prayer (1-2 minutes)

Dear God, you alone have put us in this time and at this place for your purpose. Help us live up to the tasks you set before us. Help us stand tall for what is right and godly. Give us the courage to seize the moment. Give us patience to offer sacrificial love. But Lord, there are some times we don't have the answers and can't see what is best. In those times, help us turn to you to seek your guidance and wisdom. Help us not be so conceited that we think we are your only witnesses. Let us leave now with a new sense of humility and gratitude for your love for us. In Jesus' name, amen.

Session 3

God Finds the Lost and Celebrates with Joy:
The Lost Sheep, the Lost Coin, and the Lost Son

Leader Preparation

Read chapter 3 in *How God Takes Our Little and Makes It Much*. Look through this session and decide which discussion questions will work best for your group. If the suggested questions need modification, please feel free to make the desired changes.

Leader Extra

Shepherds: According to *The New Interpreter's Dictionary of the Bible*, biblical references to shepherding reflect the fact that sheep and goats were a primary source of food, wool, and hides. Accordingly, livestock were a considerable component of family wealth. As a profession, shepherding is extremely ancient. The book of Genesis describes Abel as a keeper of sheep whose offering pleases God (Genesis 4:2-4). Later prophets frequently denounced national leaders as unfaithful shepherds who abused the flocks in their care (Isaiah 56:11; Jeremiah 12:10; 23:1-2; 50:6; Ezekiel 34:2-10; Zechariah 10:2-3). Ironically, God threatens through the prophet Zechariah to punish his people by raising up worthless shepherds who will bring them to ruin (Zechariah 11:15-17). Yet the prophets also promise that God will raise up faithful shepherds for his people (Jeremiah 3:15; 23:4). They also foretold that one day,

God himself will once more shepherd the nation (Isaiah 40:11).

Denarii were Roman silver coins. Throughout the New Testament denarii are referred to as an equivalent of payment for daily wages. So in our world if a person earns $100 a day, the woman in Luke 15 had a total of $1,000 and had lost $100—a sizable amount for us as well.

Inheritance in the story of the Prodigal Son should be read with the Old Testament traditions in mind. The promise of "inheriting the land" not only related to actual property but being chosen to inherit as well, that is, being one of the chosen people. In 1 Peter the believers are called and chosen sojourners in a foreign land who await their inheritance that is "kept in heaven" for them (1 Peter 1:4).

As you prepare for this session, reflect on what it means to find joy in finding your heart's desire. Take this study as an opportunity to celebrate the members of your group and the gifts that they each bring. Consider how each person enriches your life and enhances your spiritual journey.

Getting Started

Sharing Prayers and Concerns (5-7 minutes)

Opening Prayer (1-2 minutes)

Dear God, we praise you for being the kind of God who finds us when we are lost, who redeems us when we sin, who restores us when we are broken, and who loves us when we are unlovely. Thank you for sending Jesus, who gave his life for us and our salvation. Because of Jesus we can have eternal life beginning right now, here. We pray for those we have mentioned. Provide for their needs and help us do our part to bring health and wholeness to our world. In Jesus' name, amen.

Introduction of Study (2-3 minutes)

To the leader: Take a few minutes to introduce this session.

In this chapter, Dr. Moore has four points about being lost. First, we can get lost by wandering off. Second, we can get lost by being led astray by others. Third, we can get lost when we run away. And fourth, we can get lost in our resentment. This session focuses on three of Jesus' parables: the Lost Sheep, the Lost Coin, and the Lost Son, known as the Prodigal. But for whatever reason a person is lost, we can always count on God to come looking for us, not to punish us but to rejoice with us when we are found.

Play the DVD: Session 3 (5-10 minutes)

Icebreaker (10 minutes)

Share a time when you got lost, for example, when you were a child or on a trip. Share a time when you lost something valuable. What did you have to do to find it?

Scripture Reading (3-5 minutes)

Luke 15

Now all the tax collectors and sinners were coming near to listen to him. And the Pharisees and the scribes were grumbling and saying, "This fellow welcomes sinners and eats with them."

So he told them this parable: "Which one of you, having a hundred sheep and losing one of them, does not leave the ninety-nine in the wilderness and go after the one that is lost until he finds it? When he has found it, he lays it on his shoulders and rejoices. And when he comes home, he calls together his friends and neighbors, saying to them, 'Rejoice with me, for I have found my sheep that was lost.' Just so, I tell you, there will be more joy in heaven over one sinner who repents than over ninety-nine righteous persons who need no repentance.

"Or what woman having ten silver coins, if she loses one of them, does not light a lamp, sweep the house, and search carefully until she finds it? When she has found it, she calls together her friends and neighbors, saying, 'Rejoice with me, for I have found the coin that I had lost.' Just so, I tell you, there is joy in the presence of the angels of God over one sinner who repents."

Then Jesus said, "There was a man who had two sons. The younger of them said to his father, 'Father, give me the share of the property that will belong to me.' So he divided his property between them. A few days later the younger son gathered all he had and traveled to a distant country, and there he squandered his property in dissolute living. When he had spent everything, a severe famine took place throughout that country, and he began to be in need. So he went and hired himself out to one of the citizens of that country, who sent him to his fields to feed the pigs. He would gladly have filled himself with the pods that the pigs were eating; and no one gave him anything. But when he came to himself he said, 'How many of my father's hired hands have bread enough and to spare, but here I am dying of hunger! I will get up and go to my father, and I will say to him, "Father, I have sinned against heaven and before you; I am no longer worthy to be called your son; treat me like one of your hired hands." ' So he set off and went to his father. But while he was still far off, his father saw him and was filled with compassion; he ran and put his arms around him and kissed him. Then the son said to him, 'Father, I have sinned against heaven and before you; I am no longer worthy to be called your son.' But the father said to his slaves, 'Quickly, bring out a robe—the best one—and put it on him; put a ring on his finger and sandals on his feet. And get the fatted calf and kill it, and let us eat and celebrate;

for this son of mine was dead and is alive again; he was lost and is found!' And they began to celebrate.

"Now his elder son was in the field; and when he came and approached the house, he heard music and dancing. He called one of the slaves and asked what was going on. He replied, 'Your brother has come, and your father has killed the fatted calf, because he has got him back safe and sound.' Then he became angry and refused to go in. His father came out and began to plead with him. But he answered his father, 'Listen! For all these years I have been working like a slave for you, and I have never disobeyed your command; yet you have never given me even a young goat so that I might celebrate with my friends. But when this son of yours came back, who has devoured your property with prostitutes, you killed the fatted calf for him!' Then the father said to him, 'Son, you are always with me, and all that is mine is yours. But we had to celebrate and rejoice, because this brother of yours was dead and has come to life; he was lost and has been found.' "

Luke 5:29-39

Then Levi gave a great banquet for him in his house; and there was a large crowd of tax collectors and others sitting at the table with them. The Pharisees and their scribes were complaining to his disciples, saying, "Why do you eat and drink with tax collectors and sinners?"

Jesus answered, "Those who are well have no need of a physician, but those who are sick; I have come to call not the righteous but sinners to repentance."

Then they said to him, "John's disciples, like the disciples of the Pharisees, frequently fast and pray, but your disciples eat and drink." Jesus said to them, "You cannot make wedding guests fast while the bridegroom is with them, can you? The days will come when the bridegroom will be taken away from them, and then they will fast in those days." He also told them a parable: "No one tears a piece from a new garment and sews it on an old garment; otherwise the new will be torn, and the piece from the new will not match the old. And no one puts new wine into old wineskins; otherwise the new wine will burst the skins and will be spilled, and the skins will be destroyed. But new wine must be put into fresh wineskins. And no one after drinking old wine desires new wine, but says, 'The old is good.'"

2 Corinthians 7:1-13

Since we have these promises, beloved, let us cleanse ourselves from every defilement of body and of spirit, making holiness perfect in the fear of God.

Make room in your hearts for us; we have wronged no one, we have corrupted no one, we have taken advantage of no one. I do not say this to condemn you, for I said before that you are in our hearts, to die together and to live together. I often boast about you; I have great pride in you; I am filled with consolation; I am overjoyed in all our affliction.

For even when we came into Macedonia, our bodies had no rest, but we were afflicted in every way—disputes without and fears within. But God, who consoles the downcast, consoled us by the arrival of Titus, and not only by his coming, but also by the consolation with which he was consoled about you, as he told us of your longing, your mourning, your zeal for me, so that I rejoiced still more. For even if I made you sorry with my letter, I do not regret it (though I did regret it, for I see that I grieved you with that letter, though only briefly). Now I rejoice, not because you were grieved, but because your grief led to repentance; for you felt a godly grief, so that you were not harmed in any way by us. For godly grief produces a repentance that leads to salvation and brings no regret, but worldly grief produces death. For see what earnestness this godly grief has produced in you, what eagerness to clear yourselves, what indignation, what alarm, what longing, what zeal, what punishment! At every point you have proved yourselves guiltless in the matter. So although I wrote to you, it was not on account of the one who did the wrong, nor on account of the one who was wronged, but in order that your zeal for us might be made known to you before God. In this we find comfort.

In addition to our own consolation, we rejoiced still more at the joy of Titus, because his mind has been set at rest by all of you.

Group Discussion (20-25 minutes)

1. Share what precautions you take to keep from getting lost. On a trip, for example, do you have a GPS? Do you use internet maps? Do you carry paper maps with you? What makes for a good map?

2. Have you or someone you know ever drifted in relationship with God? What was it like? What made you or that person turn around?

3. According to Alcoholics Anonymous, people have to hit rock bottom before they are willing to change their drinking behavior. In your experience, do people really have to be so desperate before they will change for the better?

4. Dr. Moore says that religion is akin to "friendship with God." Name the characteristics you find appealing in your friends. Have the class make a list. Which of these characteristics apply to Jesus? How many apply to you?

5. Spend a few minutes talking about what true friendship is. How good a friend are you to God? How much time do you spend in prayer, study, mission, and worship? Make a commitment as a class to spend more time with God.

6. Jesus talked about his disciples as his friends. Share your favorite story in the Bible about Jesus or share your favorite story that Jesus told. What does it say about Jesus? What kinds of people were in his audience, the true believers, the skeptics, the ignorant, the powerful, the outcast? If you had been there, what group would you have been in? Do you think that Jesus had a sense of humor, a sense of wonder, or a sense of amusement? Do you think that Jesus was savvy about people? Why or why not? What kinds of qualities did Jesus value in his disciples?

7. No one wants to think that they can be led astray easily, but it happens. Share a time when you or someone you know hung out with the wrong crowd. Is there a place in your life where you need to repent?

8. No question, some people have had bad experiences with church. How welcoming is your church? If the church is the body of Christ on Earth, how good is your church at finding lost souls and leading them back home to God?

9. Reread the story of the Prodigal Son (Luke 15:11-32). With which character in the story do you most identify: the younger son, the elder brother, the father, the servants, the fatted calf, someone else? Why?

10. In biblical times, who you ate with said something about who you were. Who is welcome in your home, at your dinner table? Do you like to be the host?

11. When we are found, God wants us to celebrate. What are the marks of a successful party? How joyous is your church worship?

12. Plan a class party for fun and fellowship.

Closing Prayer (1-2 minutes)

Dear God, we thank you for your ever-seeking love. And we admit that when we are found by you, it feels good to be in your presence. We acknowledge our continued need for your love and mercy. Help us find ways to extend that love and mercy through our hospitality at church and in our homes. Let people see us as kind and loving witnesses for you. Let us depart from this place refreshed and renewed, with a right spirit within us. To you be the glory and honor. In Jesus' name, amen.

Session 4

God Takes a Fisherman and Makes a Disciple for All People: The Story of Peter

Leader Preparation

Read chapter 4 in *How God Takes Our Little and Makes It Much*. Look through this session and decide which discussion questions will work best for your group. If the suggested questions need modification, please feel free to make the desired changes.

Leader Extra

Peter: According to *The New Interpreter's Dictionary of the Bible*, Peter is mentioned 155 times in the New Testament. He was a prominent disciple of Jesus and known today to Christians everywhere. A synthesis of biblical stories provides us with a familiar picture. Peter and his brother, Andrew, were fishermen. Actually, Peter's name was Simon (Matthew 4:18) or Simeon (Acts 15:14; 2 Peter 1:1). He is also called "bar Jonah" or "son of Jonah." Jesus nicknamed him "Peter," which means "rock."

As fishermen, Peter and his family lived in Capernaum, which is on the Sea of Galilee. The New Testament portrays Peter as the most outspoken of the twelve disciples, eager to raise questions and objections. He confesses Jesus to be the Messiah, but refuses to accept Jesus' prediction of suffering (Mark 8:27-33). Various stories often show Peter to be impulsive, leading into the sea, even trying to walk on water like Jesus

(Matthew 14:22-23). He followed people who arrested Jesus to the high priest's courtyard, but he became frightened when his identity as a disciple was suspected and then he denied his association with Jesus altogether (Mark 14:66-72; John 18:25-27). Thus the Gospels consistently depict Peter as a person eager to follow Jesus but often fearful, or initially unaware, of the costs. He is earnest in following Jesus, but he stumbles and falls, needing the love and grace of Jesus to move on.

As you reflect on the upcoming lesson, examine your own earnestness in following Jesus. Where have you succeeded? How have you failed? Where have you been impulsive? Where have you been too cautious? When have you been fearful of being discovered as being a follower of Jesus? But also where have you received the love and forgiveness of Jesus? What obstacles are in your way as you prepare today? How can you be a better leader for your small group?

Getting Started

Sharing Prayers and Concerns (5-7 minutes)

Opening Prayer (1-2 minutes)

Dear God, we confess that most of the time we are in too much of a hurry. Help us slow down and focus on you for these next moments. Watch over us and our loved ones. Touch those we have mentioned who need you in a special way. May the dove of your Spirit rest upon us as we discuss and learn more how you can turn our little into much. In Jesus' name, amen.

Introduction of Study (2-3 minutes)

To the leader: Take a few minutes to introduce this session.

In this session, Dr. Moore gives us a method to help in all our Bible study. Beginning with what we see physically, what did we feel emotionally and what did we learn spiritually? That is, what do we learn about God? Using this method, this study looks at the story of Peter in John 21:1-19. Peter's story, like many of ours, is about forgiveness and resurrection. Christ conquers death, but he also resurrects us. He gives to us new life.

Play the DVD: Session 4 (5-10 minutes)

Icebreaker (10 minutes)

Share a story about eating together as a family. Or share what your favorite meal is.

Scripture Reading (3-5 minutes)

John 6:22-40

The next day the crowd that had stayed on the other side of the sea saw that there had been only one boat there. They also saw that Jesus had not got into the boat with his disciples, but that his disciples had gone away alone. Then some boats from Tiberias came near the place where they had eaten the bread after the Lord had given thanks. So when the crowd saw that neither Jesus nor his disciples were there, they themselves got into the boats and went to Capernaum looking for Jesus.

When they found him on the other side of the sea, they said to him, "Rabbi, when did you come here?" Jesus answered them, "Very truly, I tell you, you are looking for me, not because you saw signs, but because you ate your fill of the loaves. Do not work for the food that perishes, but for the food that endures for eternal life, which the Son of Man will give you. For it is on him that God the Father has set his seal." Then they said to him, "What must we do to perform the works of God?" Jesus answered them, "This is the work of God, that you believe in him whom he has sent." So they said to him, "What sign are you going to give us then, so that we may see it and believe you? What work are you performing? Our ancestors ate the manna in the wilderness; as it is written, 'He gave them bread from heaven to eat.'" Then Jesus said to them, "Very truly, I tell you, it was not Moses who gave you the bread from heaven, but it is my Father who gives you the true bread from heaven. For the bread of God is that which comes down from heaven and gives life to the world." They said to him, "Sir, give us this bread always."

Jesus said to them, "I am the bread of life. Whoever comes to me will never be hungry, and whoever believes in me will never be thirsty. But I said to you that you have seen me and yet do not believe. Everything that the

Father gives me will come to me, and anyone who comes to me I will never drive away; for I have come down from heaven, not to do my own will, but the will of him who sent me. And this is the will of him who sent me, that I should lose nothing of all that he has given me, but raise it up on the last day. This is indeed the will of my Father, that all who see the Son and believe in him may have eternal life; and I will raise them up on the last day."

John 13:1-20

Now before the festival of the Passover, Jesus knew that his hour had come to depart from this world and go to the Father. Having loved his own who were in the world, he loved them to the end. The devil had already put it into the heart of Judas son of Simon Iscariot to betray him. And during supper Jesus, knowing that the Father had given all things into his hands, and that he had come from God and was going to God, got up from the table, took off his outer robe, and tied a towel around himself. Then he poured water into a basin and began to wash the disciples' feet and to wipe them with the towel that was tied around him. He came to Simon Peter, who said to him, "Lord, are you going to wash my feet?" Jesus answered, "You do not know now what I am doing, but later you will understand." Peter said to him, "You will never wash my feet." Jesus answered, "Unless I wash you, you have no share with me." Simon

Peter said to him, "Lord, not my feet only but also my hands and my head!" Jesus said to him, "One who has bathed does not need to wash, except for the feet, but is entirely clean. And you are clean, though not all of you." For he knew who was to betray him; for this reason he said, "Not all of you are clean."

After he had washed their feet, had put on his robe, and had returned to the table, he said to them, "Do you know what I have done to you? You call me Teacher and Lord—and you are right, for that is what I am. So if I, your Lord and Teacher, have washed your feet, you also ought to wash one another's feet. For I have set you an example, that you also should do as I have done to you. Very truly, I tell you, servants are not greater than their master, nor are messengers greater than the one who sent them. If you know these things, you are blessed if you do them. I am not speaking of all of you; I know whom I have chosen. But it is to fulfill the scripture, 'The one who ate my bread has lifted his heel against me.' I tell you this now, before it occurs, so that when it does occur, you may believe that I am he. Very truly, I tell you, whoever receives one whom I send receives me; and whoever receives me receives him who sent me."

John 21:1-19

After these things Jesus showed himself again to the disciples by the Sea of Tiberias; and he showed himself in this way. Gathered there together were Simon Peter, Thomas called the Twin, Nathanael of Cana in Galilee, the sons of Zebedee, and two others of his disciples. Simon Peter said to them, "I am going fishing." They said to him, "We will go with you." They went out and got into the boat, but that night they caught nothing.

Just after daybreak, Jesus stood on the beach; but the disciples did not know that it was Jesus. Jesus said to them, "Children, you have no fish, have you?" They answered him, "No." He said to them, "Cast the net to the right side of the boat, and you will find some." So they cast it, and now they were not able to haul it in because there were so many fish. That disciple whom Jesus loved said to Peter, "It is the Lord!" When Simon Peter heard that it was the Lord, he put on some clothes, for he was naked, and jumped into the sea. But the other disciples came in the boat, dragging the net full of fish, for they were not far from the land, only about a hundred yards off.

When they had gone ashore, they saw a charcoal fire there, with fish on it, and bread. Jesus said to them, "Bring some of the fish that you have just caught." So Simon Peter went aboard and hauled the net ashore, full of large fish, a hundred fifty-three of them; and though there were so many, the net was not torn. Jesus said to them, "Come and have breakfast." Now none of the disciples dared to ask him, "Who are you?" because they knew it was the Lord. Jesus came and took the bread and gave it to them, and did the same with the fish. This was now the third time that Jesus appeared to the disciples after he was raised from the dead.

When they had finished breakfast, Jesus said to Simon Peter, "Simon son of John, do you love me more than these?" He said to him, "Yes, Lord; you know that I love you." Jesus said to him, "Feed my lambs." A second time he said to him, "Simon son of John, do you love me?" He said to him, "Yes, Lord; you know that I love you." Jesus said to him, "Tend my sheep." He said to him the third time, "Simon son of John, do you love me?" Peter felt hurt because he said to him the third time, "Do you love me?" And he said to him, "Lord, you know everything; you know that I love you." Jesus said to him, "Feed my sheep. Very truly, I tell you, when you were younger, you used to fasten your own belt and to go wherever you wished. But when you grow old, you will stretch out your hands, and someone else will fasten a belt around you and take you where you do not wish to go." (He said this to indicate the kind of death by which he would glorify God.) After this he said to him, "Follow me."

Group Discussion (20-25 minutes)

1. Reread John 13:1-20 or John 21:1-19 using Dr. Moore's three questions:

What did you see physically? What did you feel emotionally? What did you learn spiritually? Write the answers so that the whole class can see and make a master list from everyone's answers.

2. Read the scriptures again and answer these questions: Which scene or setting do you recall most vividly? Which characters stand out in your mind? Which physical objects do you remember most strongly? Write the answers so that the whole class can see and make a master list from everyone's answers.

3. Look once again at the scriptures and answer these questions as a class: Where was sin occurring in this story? Where did we see grace? Did we see the Christ-event here? Did we see death and resurrection; that is, did we see someone dying to an old, inauthentic way of living—and emerging into a new way of life, from "brokenness to wholeness"?

4. Would this series of questions be helpful to you when you study other Bible passages? How?

5. For some people it is easier to be a leader than a follower. For others, it is easier to be a follower than a leader. If you had to choose, which do you prefer being—a leader or a follower?

6. What are some characteristics of a good leader? Of a good follower? What are some places where people learn how to lead and follow?

7. How can your church offer opportunities to help persons be better followers and leaders?

8. In our society, physically touching someone can be risky or even threatening. Given our circumstances, how can we touch people appropriately?

9. Who do you know that serve people as Jesus did when he washed the disciples' feet? Who are the servant leaders that you know? How does a person become a servant leader? Are there opportunities for servant leadership in your church, at your job, in your home?

Closing Prayer (1-2 minutes)

Dear God, you are always there to touch us at the point of our deepest need. You are more willing to help us than we are to ask for help. You even washed the dusty feet of the disciples. Help us be more like you, serving others. Help us understand that it takes strength to serve as you serve. Give us that strength and confidence. But Lord, sometimes it is hard to ask for help. Banish our pride so that we can be refreshed with your overflowing grace. Free us for joyful obedience. As we leave this place, let us take with us the joy of your salvation as we live, hope, and love all of God's people. In Jesus' name, amen.

Session 5

God Takes Our Little and Makes It Much: The Story of the Church

Leader Preparation

Read chapter 5 in *How God Takes Our Little and Makes It Much*. Look through this session and decide which discussion questions will work best for your group. If the suggested questions need modification, please feel free to make the desired changes.

Leader Extra

The Church: According to *The New Interpreter's Dictionary of the Bible*, the church is the community gathered in Jesus' name to worship God and serve others. Rooted in the Jesus movement, the church took shape through faith in the saving significance of Jesus' death and resurrection, and found expression in various faith communities. The books of the New Testament bear witness to the unity and diversity of church life and organization.

Although the word *church* does not appear in every book of the New Testament, the concept of church is reflected in each of the New Testament's twenty-seven books. Throughout the New Testament, *church* is a gathering or assembly of those "called out," as the Greek etymology of the work *ekklesia* signifies. Those who are called out are called to follow Jesus, to serve and witness to others. According to various New Testament writers, what allowed the church of Jesus

Christ to grow and flourish was the power of the Holy Spirit. Paul insisted that each Christian had received the Holy Spirit and was obligated to use the gifts of the Spirit for the common good and for building up the body of Christ (1 Corinthians 12:7).

Earliest Christianity was a missionary religion. The basis for such activity was Jesus himself, who worked as a traveling preacher and teacher. But the decisive elements in the emergence of the church were the resurrection of Jesus Christ and the influence of the Holy Spirit. Thus, teachings about the resurrection, Jesus, and the Holy Spirit were central to early Christians' beliefs and formed the substance of the church's earliest core teachings.

As you prepare for this small-group session, what are your core beliefs? What core teachings are reflected in this study? What is at the core of your practice of Christianity in your daily life? When the small-group members see you, do they feel the presence and love of Christ radiating through you to them? Think about how you can show Christ's love in more effective and tangible ways.

Getting Started

Sharing Prayers and Concerns (5-7 minutes)

Opening Prayer (1-2 minutes)

Dear God, you are the light of the world. For this we praise and thank you. You give us joy and peace. For this we praise and thank you. You give us your abiding presence. For this we praise and thank you. Now help us focus on you, so that we may deepen and enrich our gratitude and thankfulness. Be with those we have mentioned who need you in a special way this week and bless us now as we lean in to listen for your voice. In Jesus' name, amen.

Introduction of Study (2-3 minutes)

To the leader: Take a few minutes to introduce this session.

When we read about the disciples in Acts 2, we find that they feel spiritually bankrupt, inadequate, and unprepared. They feel that they do not have much to bring to the table or to the altar. But then God said: "Let's put it all together! Let's pool our resources! Bring what you have and I'll take care of the rest!" In this story of the birthday of the church, Dr. Moore helps us understand how the Holy Spirit was at work and how the Holy Spirit continues to remind us that the Holy Spirit united people and that we should live in that inclusive spirit, that the Holy Spirit excites people and that we should live in that exciting spirit; and that the Holy Spirit invites us and that we should live in that inviting spirit.

Being the church as God envisions it means that we, together, live with an inclusive, exciting, and inviting spirit.

Play the DVD: Session 5 (5-10 minutes)

Icebreaker (10 minutes)

Share your favorite thing about your church and your small group. Share why you chose your church.

Scripture Reading (3-5 minutes)

Acts 2

When the day of Pentecost had come, they were all together in one place. And suddenly from heaven there came a sound like the rush of a violent wind, and it filled the entire house where they were sitting. Divided tongues, as of fire, appeared among them, and a tongue rested on each of them. All of them were filled with the Holy Spirit and began to speak in other languages, as the Spirit gave them ability.

Now there were devout Jews from every nation under heaven living in Jerusalem. And at this sound the crowd gathered and was bewildered, because each one heard them speaking in the native language of each. Amazed and astonished, they asked, "Are not all these who are speaking Galileans? And how is it that we hear, each of us, in our own native language? Parthians, Medes, Elamites, and residents of Mesopotamia, Judea and Cappadocia, Pontus and Asia, Phrygia and Pamphylia, Egypt and the parts of Libya belonging to Cyrene, and visitors from Rome, both Jews and proselytes, Cretans and Arabs—in our own languages we hear them speaking about God's deeds of power." All were amazed and perplexed, saying to one another, "What does this mean?" But others sneered and said, "They are filled with new wine."

But Peter, standing with the eleven, raised his voice and addressed them, "Men of Judea and all who live in Jerusalem, let this be known to you, and listen to what I say. Indeed, these are not drunk, as you suppose, for it is only nine o'clock in the morning. No, this is what was spoken through the prophet Joel:

'In the last days it will be, God declares,
   that I will pour out my Spirit upon all flesh,
      and your sons and your daughters shall prophesy,
   and your young men shall see visions,
      and your old men shall dream dreams.
Even upon my slaves, both men and women,
   in those days I will pour out my Spirit;
      and they shall prophesy.
And I will show portents in the heaven above
   and signs on the earth below,
      blood, and fire, and smoky mist.
The sun shall be turned to darkness
   and the moon to blood,
      before the coming of the Lord's great and
         glorious day.

Then everyone who calls on the name of the Lord shall be saved.'

"You that are Israelites, listen to what I have to say: Jesus of Nazareth, a man attested to you by God with deeds of power, wonders, and signs that God did through him among you, as you yourselves know—this man, handed over to you according to the definite plan and foreknowledge of God, you crucified and killed by the hands of those outside the law. But God raised him up, having freed him from death, because it was impossible for him to be held in its power. For David says concerning him,

'I saw the Lord always before me,
for he is at my right hand so that I will not
be shaken;
therefore my heart was glad, and my tongue rejoiced;
moreover my flesh will live in hope.
For you will not abandon my soul to Hades,
or let your Holy One experience corruption.
You have made known to me the ways of life;
you will make me full of gladness with your
presence.'

"Fellow Israelites, I may say to you confidently of our ancestor David that he both died and was buried, and his tomb is with us to this day. Since he was a prophet, he knew that God had sworn with an oath to him that he would put one of his descendants on his throne. Foreseeing this, David spoke of the resurrection of the Messiah, saying,

'He was not abandoned to Hades,

nor did his flesh experience corruption.'

This Jesus God raised up, and of that all of us are witnesses. Being therefore exalted at the right hand of God, and having received from the Father the promise of the Holy Spirit, he has poured out this that you both see and hear. For David did not ascend into the heavens, but he himself says,

'The Lord said to my Lord,

"Sit at my right hand,

until I make your enemies your footstool." '

Therefore let the entire house of Israel know with certainty that God has made him both Lord and Messiah, this Jesus whom you crucified."

Now when they heard this, they were cut to the heart and said to Peter and to the other apostles, "Brothers, what should we do?" Peter said to them, "Repent, and be baptized every one of you in the name of Jesus Christ so that your sins may be forgiven; and you will receive the gift of the Holy Spirit. For the promise is for you, for your children, and for all who are far away, everyone whom the Lord our God calls to him." And he testified with many other arguments and exhorted them, saying,

"Save yourselves from this corrupt generation." So those who welcomed his message were baptized, and that day about three thousand persons were added. They devoted themselves to the apostles' teaching and fellowship, to the breaking of bread and the prayers.

Awe came upon everyone, because many wonders and signs were being done by the apostles. All who believed were together and had all things in common; they would sell their possessions and goods and distribute the proceeds to all, as any had need. Day by day, as they spent much time together in the temple, they broke bread at home and ate their food with glad and generous hearts, praising God and having the goodwill of all the people. And day by day the Lord added to their number those who were being saved.

Matthew 23:16-19

"Woe to you, blind guides, who say, 'Whoever swears by the sanctuary is bound by nothing, but whoever swears by the gold of the sanctuary is bound by the oath.' You blind fools! For which is greater, the gold or the sanctuary that has made the gold sacred? And you say, 'Whoever swears by the altar is bound by nothing, but whoever swears by the gift that is on the altar is bound by the oath.' How blind you are! For which is greater, the gift or the altar that makes the gift sacred?"

Group Discussion (20-25 minutes)

1. Share how you came to Christ.

2. As the disciples waited in the Upper Room, Acts 1:1-4, they devoted themselves to prayer. How often do you pray? Do you have a special time or place where prayer is most meaningful? How often do you pray with your family, friends?

3. Have you ever had a prayer partner? Share an experience when you prayed with someone else and it was meaningful.

4. The disciples waited because Jesus promised that he would send the Holy Spirit. What promises of God do you count on in your daily life?

5. On a scale from one to ten (one being lowest and ten being highest), rate your church on these things: How loving is your church? How welcoming is your church? How generous is your church? How great is the worship at your church? How mission-oriented is your church? How spiritually fruitful is your church? Is your church growing in its love and service? How can your church help you become more welcoming, generous, worshipful, mission-oriented, and spiritually fruitful?

6. Is your life marked by the fruits of the Spirit as found in Galatians 5:22-23? Where are you most fruitful: love, joy, peace, patience, kindness, generosity, faith-

fulness, gentleness, self-control? Where would you like to be more fruitful?

7. The church is where we actively engage in the love of Christ in the world. In what ways is your church being a light to the world? Who has been helped because your church was there and cared?

8. If all power on heaven and earth was available to you, what would your church look like? What outreach would you do? Where would your church be located? What kinds of people would attend? Who would be your leaders? What kind of witness would you give?

9. United Methodist churches are connected to one another in purpose, mission, and ministry. How does your church take advantage of your connection to other United Methodist churches in your district, conference, jurisdiction? How does your church connect with other churches in your community? Do you think it is important?

10. Self-denial and simple living are messages that are often tough for people to hear, much less do. Share your thoughts and feelings about what it might mean for you to live more simply or with greater self-denial. Is this or should this be a part of Christian witness?

11. Dr. Moore reminds us that the Holy Spirit inspires and excites us to reach out in God's name. How do you feel about this? Do you agree? Why or why not?

12. If the purpose of the church is to proclaim the good news, how is your church doing? How can you proclaim the good news in your own life? What is the difference between witnessing with your life and witnessing with your words? What is the most effective witness for you?

13. Reflect back about your time with this study. What was most helpful? What was a waste of time? Did it help or hinder you on your spiritual journey? Are you better able to live a grace-filled life? Is your heart warmed and are your hands active in mission?

14. Spend a few moments talking about what you would like to study next.

Closing Prayer (1-2 minutes)

Dear God, as we close this study, we confess that we still have a lot to learn about you. We still have a long way to travel to get to the place we need to be. We long to be your faithful witnesses. Thank you for your grace. Give us the strength, courage, and perseverance to bring others to you. Thank you for the opportunity to reach out to others. We realize that the good news is meant to be shared. Empower us be truly excited about our faith and live in joyful obedience. In Jesus' name, amen.

Session 6

God Takes Mere Sinners and Makes Us *More* than Conquerors

Leader Preparation

Read chapter 6 in *How God Takes Our Little and Makes It Much*. Look through this session and decide which discussion questions will work best for your group. If the suggested questions need modification, please feel free to make the desired changes.

Leader Extra

Conquerors: In English, *to conquer* has the sense of overpowering something or someone to the point of surrender. According to *The New Interpreter's Dictionary of the Bible*, in the Old Testament, various verbs or phrases are translated as *conquer*, such as words also meaning "to smite" or "to dispossess," or "to prevail" as in battle. But the word also suggests endurance. In Revelation, conquerors lay down their lives like the Lamb (Revelation 7:9-17). In the Johannine theology of the New Testament, the contest is spiritual (John 16:33), and those who conquer evil are usually engaged in an internalized battle (1 John 2:13).

While New Testament texts reveal the evil and demonic qualities of the Roman Empire in particular, they also anticipate and imagine its imminent downfall. The question is: How are believers to live in their everyday world of toil and trouble? In many of the New

Testament writings, what emerges is an ambivalent mixture of pragmatic cooperation to ensure survival, nonviolent but active resistance expressive of faithfulness to God's purposes, and the shaping of alternative communities with practices and commitments that differ from imperial ways.

A dramatic difference in how the Romans viewed religion from most people today is that there was no attempt to separate the affairs of state from religious practice. Religion served as the glue that held together the many forces that controlled society, so it was only natural that all facets of government included regular interaction with religious institutions and rituals. In many ways, military success was at the foundation of the power and influence of the Roman Empire, and that success was understood to be due to the favor of the gods. The fusing of religious and political power was most obvious in the person of the Roman Emperor. Prayers and offerings were made on a regular basis for his good health and military victory.

The very real consequences for choosing to follow Jesus highlight important lessons for us. First, they underline the power of the early Christian message and the commitment that was needed to accept and adopt it. Second, they put into high relief the amazing success of the churches in providing alternative forms of social structure and meaning for those who chose to join. Finally, they lead to an understanding of how quickly a system of religious ritual, calendar, social hierarchy, and governmental activities came to dominate the government, even after the fall of the Roman Empire.

As you prepare for this final session, reflect on the commitments needed to be a Christian today. How are we able to live in our everyday world of toil and trouble as faithful witnesses to the power and love of God? Reflect on what you have learned about the Bible, yourself, and your group members during this study. What are your next steps on your spiritual journey?

Consider planning a group activity to celebrate what you have learned about the Bible and one another. Give thanks for the presence of God in your life and in the life of your group.

Getting Started

Sharing Prayers and Concerns (5-7 minutes)

Opening Prayer (1-2 minutes)

Dear God, we thank you for the guidance of the Bible and what it means to Christians all around the world. Yet we confess that we haven't read it as we should and that we don't understand it as we might. Prepare our hearts and minds to be more receptive to your word. Let us not use the Bible to divide us or as a weapon to enable conflict. Lord, we long to experience you and hear the good news. Please be with those we have lifted up in prayer and help us turn to you in our hour of need. In Jesus' name, amen.

Introduction of Study (2-3 minutes)

To the leader: Take a few minutes to introduce this session.

In this final session, Dr. Moore calls us to daily move forward in our spiritual journey. He reminds us that Christ shows us, as a baby in a manger and as a Savior on a cross, that the happy people, the fulfilled people, the genuine people, are not bullies, not power mongers, not selfish people, not mean-spirited people. Christ is always calling us to be "more than conquerors," to be merciful, humble, and thoughtful, to be considerate, patient and kind, forgiving and loving. Of course, there are times when we have to defend ourselves and others, but Christ is teaching us to walk through life gently and graciously so that we don't selfishly elbow other people out of our way or push or shove or grab or possess.

As Christians, we are called to be more than conquerors in our homes with our family, our significant others, and, yes, with God.

Play the DVD: Session 6 (5-10 minutes)

Icebreaker (10 minutes)

Share with the group a story about one of your best

friends. Where did you meet? What are your favorite things to do together? Share with the group something that you are absolutely sure of.

Plan a group party.

Scripture Reading (3-5 minutes)

Romans 8:28-39

We know that all things work together for good for those who love God, who are called according to his purpose. For those whom he foreknew he also predestined to be conformed to the image of his Son, in order that he might be the firstborn within a large family. And those whom he predestined he also called; and those whom he called he also justified; and those whom he justified he also glorified.

What then are we to say about these things? If God is for us, who is against us? He who did not withhold his own Son, but gave him up for all of us, will he not with him also give us everything else? Who will bring any charge against God's elect? It is God who justifies. Who is to condemn? It is Christ Jesus, who died, yes, who was raised, who is at the right hand of God, who indeed intercedes for us. Who will separate us from the love of Christ? Will hardship, or distress, or persecution, or famine, or nakedness, or peril, or sword? As it is written,

"For your sake we are being killed all day long;
we are accounted as sheep to be slaughtered."
No, in all these things we are more than conquerors
through him who loved us. For I am convinced that neither death, nor life, nor angels, nor rulers, nor things
present, nor things to come, nor powers, nor height,
nor depth, nor anything else in all creation, will be able
to separate us from the love of God in Christ Jesus our
Lord.

Romans 12:9-21

Let love be genuine; hate what is evil, hold fast to
what is good; love one another with mutual affection;
outdo one another in showing honor. Do not lag in zeal,
be ardent in spirit, serve the Lord. Rejoice in hope, be
patient in suffering, persevere in prayer. Contribute to
the needs of the saints; extend hospitality to strangers.

Bless those who persecute you; bless and do not curse
them. Rejoice with those who rejoice, weep with those
who weep. Live in harmony with one another; do not be
haughty, but associate with the lowly; do not claim to
be wiser than you are. Do not repay anyone evil for evil,
but take thought for what is noble in the sight of all. If
it is possible, so far as it depends on you, live peaceably
with all. Beloved, never avenge yourselves, but leave
room for the wrath of God; for it is written, "Vengeance
is mine, I will repay, says the Lord." No, "if your

enemies are hungry, feed them; if they are thirsty, give them something to drink; for by doing this you will heap burning coals on their heads." Do not be overcome by evil, but overcome evil with good.

Group Discussion (20-25 minutes)

1. Share about someone you know who has faced an illness or another difficult circumstance with courage and trust in God. What can we learn from these people?

2. Share about someone who has refused to be or become a victim. What does it mean to put your trust in God? Where is the line between leaning on God and not being responsible for your own actions?

3. Jesus was much more that a conqueror, but he was also human and suffered temptation. How well do you deal with temptation? How can someone "face down" temptation? What kinds of things tempt us?

4. The Rich Young Ruler seemingly had it all. He was successful in the eyes of the world, but Jesus saw that he was lacking. Are there places in your life where Jesus might think that you are lacking? How do you address your own weaknesses? Who do you turn to when you need help?

5. When it comes to financial giving, poorer people pay a greater percentage of their income than richer people. Why do you think that is? Why does it seem to be harder to give the more that you have?

6. Do you treat your children as well as you treat your friends? Why or why not? What is the place of discipline in raising children? What works best for your child or grandchild? How can parents show grace and mercy to their children? What is the best way to be fair and just in raising children?

7. Share a time when you were disciplined in a helpful way. In an unhelpful way?

8. Why might couples compete with each other?

9. Share a time when you had to have the last word or were in discussion when someone else had to have the last word. What does that say about that person? Do you keep a tally of who wins and who loses the arguments in your household? How often do you win? What do you get for winning?

10. We all bring gifts to God. What gifts do you bring to your church? Are you a teacher, musician, administrator, trustee, leader, prayer warrior, speaker, exhorter, servant leader, follower, listener, caregiver, planner, communicator? If you could have one job in the church, what job would you like to have? What kinds of jobs go undone in your church?

11. Is there something in your life that you need to conquer? What could be a first step toward overcoming an obstacle?

12. Why might it sometimes be easier to treat people as things rather than as people? Is there someone with whom you need to be more than a conqueror? How does it feel to be treated like a thing rather than as a person? How does it feel when you treat someone like a person rather than as a thing? What makes people treat others as things?

13. Share a time when you or someone you know was treated as a thing and not as a person.

14. Augustine, Luther, and Wesley were unsure of their salvation until they encountered the book of Romans. Although they had read the Scriptures many times, this time they heard them differently. Has there been a time in your life when the Bible made a big impact on your life? Have you ever had your heart "strangely warmed"? What does "strangely warmed" mean?

15. Are you sure of your salvation? Why or why not? We all doubt. What is the place of doubt in your faith? Is doubt always a negative? How can doubt help sharpen your faith?

16. According to 2 Timothy, the Scriptures are meant to equip you for every good work. What good work are you currently doing? What good work is your church doing? How different would your community be if your church was not there? How can your friends tell that you are a Christian?

Closing Prayer (1-2 minutes)

Dear God, inspire us to follow you more closely and love you more dearly each day. Inspire confidence and assurance in us so that we can be more faithful disciples. Empower us to put your word into action in our daily lives. Take the little faith that we have and turn it into a greater faith so that we are not just hearers of the word, but also doers of the word. Let us be more than conquerors. In Jesus' name, amen.